IF YOU MUST SPECULATE, LEARN THE RULES

If You Must Speculate, Learn the Rules

Frank J. Williams

COSIMO CLASSICS

NEW YORK

If You Must Speculate, Learn the Rules

© 2005 Cosimo, Inc.

All rights reserved. No part of this book may be used or reproduced in any manner whatsoever without prior written permission except in the case of brief quotations embodied in critical articles or reviews.

For information, address:

Cosimo, P.O. Box 416
Old Chelsea Station
New York, NY 10113-0416

or visit our website at:
www.cosimobooks.com

If You Must Speculate, Learn the Rules originally published by The Fraser Publishing Company in 1930.

Library of Congress Cataloging-in-Publication Data

A catalog record for this book is available from the Library of Congress

Cover design by www.wiselephant.com

ISBN: 1-59605-649-5

FOREWORD

It was generally believed that the market crash of 1929 taught the speculative public such a severe lesson that a generation would pass before a new crop of speculators grew up. But you might as well tell Americans not to breathe as not to speculate. They are at it again, writing in to newspapers, tipping-agencies, and brokers' offices asking the same old questions and eager for tips. Interest in stocks is growing daily.

It is time to stop preaching to the smaller speculators and make an attempt to teach them the ropes. After all, there is no reason why they should not speculate if they can afford it. Whether we tell them they may or may not, they will anyway. Let us give them a sporting chance.

We are all gamblers at heart. We cannot be blamed for wanting to get at the best things in life in the quickest possible way. This is the spirit of America. The stock-market seems to offer the most rapid road to fortune.

The creed of the new speculator is: "I want to make a lot of money on little capital in a short time without working for it." This is just as impossible in Wall Street as it is in any other place.

Money can be made in speculation on the stock-market, but it is made slowly and only by a thoughtful and deliberate course of action. The quick profits are just froth. They arouse a fever in the blood and don't last. The worst thing that can happen to a new speculator is to make a lot of quick money on his first trade.

Haphazard dabbling in stocks by amateur traders undoubtedly is dangerous. The odds are all in favor of losing money. The risks can be greatly reduced if the trader only would make some attempt to learn the rules of the game. Driving an automobile is dangerous, and few people attempt it without first learning something of the mechanism of a car. But any death-dealing machine can be made safe through knowledge of its working parts and possibilities.

The stock-market undoubtedly is a death-dealing machine to hundreds of thousands of people financially, but only because they have yet to learn how to operate it.

New speculators are eager to learn how to make money in Wall Street. They should first try to learn how to protect the capital they already possess. The methods used by wealthy men to protect their millions can just as easily be used by small speculators to protect their hundreds or thousands.

I believe a trader first starts to make money in the market when he realizes that he is winning and losing actual currency. While he surveys his operations only as paper transactions, they mean little. The average man would be shocked if he lost a thousand dollars in cash from his pocket. It does not seem so serious when he does not actually handle the money.

The men who have rolled up fortunes in the Street can't give you rules for accumulating wealth. I have interviewed dozens of the biggest operators, and I have always asked them in vain for a formula. Most of the get-rich schemes in Wall Street are not workable for the person who has other business to attend to. Making money in the stock-market depends largely on the speculator's ability to obey certain common-sense rules.

This book has no get-rich scheme to offer. It hopes to put a red beacon light at the holes new margin traders are certain to fall into. Information is available to all today that only millionaires could get some years ago. If speculators refuse to seek this information and refuse to obey the rules of Wall Street, they have nobody to blame but themselves if they come to grief. Information is so easily obtainable today that there should be no "lambs" in Wall Street.

Many speculators "playing the market" know all the facts herein presented, but they still persist in breaking the rules, gambling on the million-to-one chance that they will be the lucky ones to make quick fortunes without working for them.

The market teaches many a lesson of life, and it is undoubtedly a hard master. One of its great commandments is: "Thou shalt not get something for nothing." For every dollar earned in the stock market *you must give a dollar's worth of time and thought. The market delights to catch the speculator in a careless or a reckless mood. If you are intelligent, the market will teach you caution and fortitude, sharpen your wits, and reduce your pride. If you are foolish and refuse to learn a lesson, it will ridicule you, laugh you to scorn, break you, and toss you on to the rubbish-heap. The stock-market is cruel, but it is glorious, representing all that we admire in the American character, courage, vitality, forethought, vision, and enterprise.*

FRANK J. WILLIAMS

CONTENTS

It Can Be Done

You need not be a millionaire to make money in the stock-market. It is possible for the "small man" in Wall Street to make money and to continue to make money. Over a period of years he can build up a comfortable stake if he obeys the rules followed by the big fellows.

This means that he must be as careful with his five hundred or five thousand dollars as the rich man is with his millions. He must view the stock-market as a big business to be treated seriously, and not as a betting arena.

He must be prepared to give a great deal of his time to a study of big business.

The information used by wealthy men as a basis of operations in the stock-market is today public property, available to all. Thousands of experts are anxious to help the small man build up his capital.

But wealthy men are satisfied to see money multiply slowly. The small trader in Wall Street is impatient to make a fortune. He wants to get rich quickly. This is natural. The wealthy man has plenty of money to live on while his capital is growing. The man of moderate means has a thousand needs for cash. He goes into the stock-market to make money to reduce the mortgage, to pay the doctor, or to buy his wife a fur coat. He cannot order his profits. The market refuses to be hurried.

The small man does not want to study carefully built-up statistics. He is not prepared to sit down patiently and wait for profits. He wants money and he wants it now. Tips, promises, false but glowing, something that will hearten him for the moment, are what he wants.

By impatience the small man defeats his own purpose and becomes a tool in the hands of the big fellows.

There is only one narrow trail leading to permanent success in the stock-market. Unless traders are prepared to climb that steep path with cautious steps, it would be better for them to stay out of Wall Street and to keep their money in the savings-bank.

The glistening broad highway in Wall Street traveled by millions leads only to false hopes and shattered dreams.

Men with the smallest amount of capital value money least. The rich man watches his dollars carefully. His poorer brother feels that his small amount is not worth conserving. This theory is true in ordinary life and particularly true in Wall Street. The average small trader takes a flyer in the market without forethought, on the theory that if he loses, he is not much out. Gambling in stocks in this happy-go-lucky, hit-or-miss style used by hundreds of thousands is a hopeless waste of time and money.

The stock-market is not a Monte Carlo. It is an important part of the nation's life. Through it flows the money that keeps the wheels of industry turning. When you buy stock, you have acquired the privilege of participating in big business.

Why buy stock without investigation?

You would not buy a house without having the title searched. Speculators using as much common sense in buying stock as in buying a house or a car would have nothing to fear in the stock-market.

The first thing the small trader in Wall Street must do is to rid his mind of the treasure-hunting idea and get down to business—big business.

Don't be ashamed of your few hundreds or thousands. The large corporations need your small capital, and they will pay you well for the loan.

MARGIN THE MINIMUM

There is nothing wrong in margin trading. It is a perfectly legitimate method of doing business very much abused.

Margin trading actually is in use in all lines of business. You buy a house on margin.

In the stock-market margin trading is recognized as a necessary part of stock distribution. The sale of stock is absolutely necessary to the economic growth of the country.

Ninety per cent of the business done on the stock exchange is for margin account. Seventy-five per cent of those using this method in the purchase of stock lose money.

Why?

Because the margin trader forgets that his margin is the minimum capital he can do business on, and that he might be asked to put up more money. He has no reserves, and his forces are wiped out in the first attack. More than a minimum amount of capital is required in any business if success is to be assured.

The average Wall Street trader takes advantage of the margin system to stretch his resources to the limit. He pushes his ship along with all canvas spread, taking no pains to keep a weather eye open.

Success in margin trading in stocks is in proportion to the care and thought given to it by speculators. The average small trader does not think. He bets, depending largely on luck and tips, and he always overbuys.

Speculation in stocks is in itself an exacting profession to which men give their lives. It is a risky side-line. Between an ordinary business and the stock-market the latter is certain to pull the stronger. Make speculation a servant, not a master. Those who dabble carelessly in the market pay dearly for their thrills.

Men have been known to turn small margin accounts into fairly large fortunes quickly. They had to quit their regular jobs to do it. One cannot serve two masters.

Trading on margin is the easiest and quickest way to make or lose money in the stock-market. Hence its popularity in America, where people demand a kick with investments.

Margin traders speculate on borrowed money. The method is enticing. Traders can buy more stock on margin than they could for cash.

Speculators trading on a marginal basis pay only part of the cost price of stock. The broker holding the stock certificates as pledge borrows the balance of the purchase-price at his bank to finance the transaction.

Suppose a prospective trader has only $2,500 to operate with. He wants to buy stock quoted at $100 a share. With his small capital he can buy outright only twenty-five shares. On margin he could buy a hundred shares. The broker most likely would ask him to put up twenty-five per cent of the total cost, or $25 a share. But this would be the minimum margin requirement. Should the market decline, the trader must put up more money immediately or be sold out.

Traders forget they are "holding the bag" and that neither the broker nor the banker has any intention of losing money on the deal. The original purchaser of the stock is liable for its full cost and pays interest on the money borrowed to help finance the transaction. Margin accounts are constantly scrutinized by the broker and the banker.

WALL STREET'S WORK

Wall Street's chief work is the manufacture and sale of bonds and stocks. After the securities have been manufactured, they pass from plane to plane until they either reach the gilt-edged investment class or sink into obscurity.

The evolution of stock from the speculative class to the investment class is called in Wall Street "seasoning."

After a public offering of stock has been made, the new-comer is often first traded in "over the counter" or in the unlisted market which underlies the stock exchanges. Here some basis for trading between buyer and seller is reached.

The unlisted market is one of Wall Street's big institutions, and in it are the keenest brains of the Street. Trading in this market is done over the telephone between the various unlisted houses. In these houses professional traders sit all day with earphones on their heads haggling over eighths and quarters, quite often with nothing to guide them but common sense and intuition. Many good stocks are never listed and their market is made "over the counter."

When a stock is listed on the New York Curb Exchange, it undergoes further process of refinement. It reaches the New York Stock Exchange, known as the Big Board, only after it has become well known.

Professional speculators and gamblers play an important part in the evolution of new shares. It is their buying and selling that gradually establishes values. They pave the way and make it safe for the genuine investor who wants to buy and hold.

The man with a small capital who wants safety and a return on his money should wait patiently until this seasoning has been accomplished before he buys stock.

Wall Street has many departments. The banks receive and pay out the nation's money and stand on top of the heap. Investment bankers manufacture the securities that are sold to the public. They bring together the corporations wishing to borrow money and that section of the public with money to lend.

Brokers, members of the exchanges, are the middlemen who handle the buying and selling orders for the bankers, and the public.

WHERE DO YOU BELONG?

Are you an investor, a speculator, or a trader? It is very important that you are classified before opening an account at the brokers. A different technique is used in each of the three groups.

Many people want to be investors, but degenerate into day-to-day traders, or gamblers, because there is nobody to guide them.

The belief is almost universal that speculation in stocks means as many transactions as possible. This belief keeps the brokers busy, but it is fallacious.

The savings of the nation should be permitted to flow evenly into business. This process goes by various names, and the people who lend money to industry are placed in different classes.

The two broad classifications are investment and speculation, but these terms are elastic.

An investor is one who buys sound securities where

he knows his principal will be safe and he will get a fair income return on his money.

The speculator is he who buys today with the hope of selling tomorrow or next month at a higher price.

The terms "investment" and "speculation" cover many subdivisions of financial practice. The investor may buy a "semi-speculative" security, which in plain English means a security with all the earmarks of safety, yet with a known risk.

A speculator may study conditions as carefully as an investor, or he may be a day-to-day trader, who is an ordinary gambler or gamester. A large majority of those who buy stocks in Wall Street belong to the latter class, whether they know it or not.

If you belong in the investment class, don't set out to buy stocks on margin.

If you have an exacting business of your own, don't try to be an active day-to-day trader.

If you believe yourself qualified to become an active gambler, be sure you know the ropes and be prepared to lose.

Don't be vague and uncertain. If you can't make up your mind, somebody will make it up for you.

Stay away from Wall Street until you are absolutely certain in your own mind that you are doing the right thing. If you go round asking people what you should do, you will run into somebody who deliberately or innocently will give you wrong advice. This will mean months of discouragement before you find yourself again.

WHO MAY SPECULATE?

Fortune is fickle and deserts the person who needs her most urgently.

The man or woman who cannot afford to lose should leave speculation alone. You cannot afford to lose if you need the money for other purposes.

The whole secret of success in stock-market speculation is picking good stocks, buying them at a reasonable price, and staying with them.

The wealthy man need never lose, because if he makes a mistake and buys at the wrong time, he can take up his stock, pay for it outright, and put it away for years if necessary.

The smaller trader who cannot afford to lose might use good judgment and pick a good stock, but he cannot stay with it. He should not buy any stock in the first place, because he is not in a position to pay for it outright. In an extended decline, when the market is driven down below levels of actual values, the small trader's resources are used up and he is sold out by the broker, usually right at the turning-point.

It is heart-breaking to hold a stock all through a break in the market, knowing that there will come a time when you cannot put up any more margin, and clinging like a drowning man to the hope that something will happen to save you. That something rarely happens. By order of some inexorable fate the market seems to decline far enough to get your last dollar and then rebounds.

This does not happen to you alone, but to hundreds

of thousands of people. Professional Wall Street, shrewd and calculating, knows that the market is full of traders who cannot afford to speculate. Their speculations are called "weak holdings." When the stock-market is puffed up by the speculation of a large number of inexperienced traders who will become panic-stricken at the first sign of trouble, it is said that stocks are in "weak hands."

Bear traders figure out fairly accurately how far the market will have to be driven down to exhaust the resources of the weak traders. They have no personal animosity towards the small traders. It is a matter of business. The bear lives by catching the stock-market in a weak position and depressing it. He makes his profits on declines. He knows that in certain circumstances by his speculative selling he can stampede the herd of frightened amateur speculators, who will do the rest of his work for him. When the last weak account has been wiped out, the bear will "cover" and the market rebounds.

The hundreds of thousands of small speculators who are wiped out in every minor swing of the stock-market believe they are victims of fate and that their losses are accidental. The disaster is a matter of cause and effect. They cannot afford to lose and therefore are certain to lose. If they could buy their stock outright when occasion arose, these margin traders could defy the bears and help turn the tables on them. The great majority of small traders break the fundamental rules of the stock-market, and they can win only by accident.

One reason it was so hard to break the speculative bubble of 1928 and 1929 was that traders were gambling on larger margins. But the bears got them in the end, and in the whirlwind decline of the fall of 1929 the largest margin was not adequate. Only those who could buy their stock outright if necessary weathered the storm.

A person has no right to speculate in securities unless he is in an assured position.

Men and women certainly should not speculate until they have paid the landlord, the butcher, and the tailor. They should have no doctor's bills or insurance premiums overdue.

The trader using for speculation money he needs is certain to lose.

It is of no use grumbling about the rights of the privileged classes and the disadvantages of the poorer classes. This is a matter of cold, hard common sense and safety. It is absolutely unsafe to gamble in stocks unless the trader can protect himself at all times. It is wiser to build up a substantial reserve before invading the stock-market than to fritter away money in hopeless attempts to beat it.

Those who have little money of their own and yet handle large sums of money belonging to other people should not speculate. The Stock Exchange rules that its members cannot accept accounts from salaried people in certain positions of trust. This is a wise ruling, as the temptations of the stock-market are sometimes too strong even for honest men.

In recent months there has been a great deal of

discussion whether women should speculate. There is no reason why women should not speculate if they keep their heads and use their own money. It was found in the big crash of 1929 that large numbers of women were gambling with their husbands' money. This practice is unsound. The greatest weakness in amateur speculators is that they don't properly value their own money. They are likely to value even less money they don't earn.

It is not hard to imagine that the practice of a married woman gambling in stocks with money given to her by her husband for household or other purposes is likely to cause great domestic unhappiness.

In advising women not to speculate wise bankers and brokers are not using sex discrimination. It is simply that a large majority of women are temperamentally and financially not yet ready to cope with the dangers of the stock-market. Women in the board rooms of brokerage houses are a common sight today, but few of them are successful, and brokers are not eager for their accounts.

Race and position are important factors in deciding who or who should not speculate in stocks. The more excitable, high-strung races make poor speculators, because they are too jumpy. Nerves are a liability in the stock-market. The more stolid thinkers are most likely to make a success of speculation.

The one exception among the more excitable races is the French, who are rated as the world's most careful speculators. The French are a thrifty race, and, once having saved money, they are very careful what they do with it. They are not given to embarking on wild ventures, but usually are satisfied with a small return with safety. The French are masters of diversification and in their investments seek safety by putting their capital to work in different directions. In other words, they dislike putting all their eggs in one basket.

The English take long chances. They are rated the most daring and enterprising speculators and the world's greatest gamblers. These qualities of the race have resulted in Britain's far-flung empire. Only Englishmen would have invested money in the out-of-the-way corners of the earth that have developed into prosperous colonies. But then the English investor does not want to see his investment turn into a gold-mine overnight. He is ready to wait five, ten, or twenty years for his reward. The English have suffered enormous individual losses because of their daring speculation, but the nation as a whole has profited by its financial policy.

The Germans are the cleverest speculators in the world, combining the English daring with the French care, and in addition having a thoroughness of method and a passion for accurate detail not found in any other race. The trouble a German will go to in investigating a situation to the smallest detail is astounding. Once in full possession of the real facts, a German will take chances with any other race.

The Dutch, of course, have developed investment

to a high art, but they are not given to taking desperate chances.

American speculators have one great fault. They are too anxious to cash in their profits. They are not prepared to wait for developments even if they are fairly sure that there will be developments. The American speculator wants action and he usually has to pay for it.

Only in America do stocks churn round so actively, and only in America do stock exchanges attempt to quote every transaction of the day on the stock ticker at the exact price at which it was made. Foreigners are astonished at the way American speculators jump in and out of the market a dozen or more times a day, and it is almost unbelievable to them that the full record of a day's transactions on the Exchange can be printed figure by figure by the close of the market or shortly afterwards.

When an American speculator buys a stock, he expects it to show a profit immediately. If it does not move right away, he grows restless and sells out and jumps into another stock that is moving. In this highly unsatisfactory process he usually misses all the profits, because it is next to impossible to guess what a stock is going to do. It is common for active speculators to buy a stock at the opening of the market and jump out again before the close because it has not moved. They have most likely sold at a loss besides paying commissions.

In the consideration of position it is safe to say that men with the most exacting professions will generally have the least success in the stock-market. They have not the time nor the inclination to make the proper study of conditions.

Doctors and dentists, for instance, are the unluckiest speculators. They have given so much time and study to their professions that they are overcredulous in the matter of stock speculation.

A doctor told me after the break in stocks in 1929 that he had lost fifty thousand dollars in the market, and that it represented years of the most exacting work and nerve-wracking surgical operations. He could give no really good reason why he bought the stocks in the first place, and he was not quite clear how it came about that he was sold out. He bought the stocks because a customers' man in a brokerage house told him to. This doctor was a brilliant surgeon, with the highest degree of intelligence.

Small tradesmen are pathetic specimens of stock speculators. They generally lose both ways, in the market, and at the store because of neglect. The small tradesman as a rule has to work in the store from early morning until late at night. His is a life of drudgery. His profits are small and he piles up capital slowly and only by the greatest thrift and economy. He is not in a position to make a study of stocks and he should not speculate. Retail tradesmen were in the market in large numbers at the time of the great crash in 1929 and they had bought mostly on the tips brought to their stores by customers and traveling salesmen.

One exception to this rule is a baker I know, who

has built up a comfortable fortune out of a very small beginning. But he is a real speculator and not a gambler. He waits patiently for the periodical bear market to come round and he will wait for years. Then, when he believes stocks are at the very bottom, he goes down to the brokerage house and buys a line of stocks he has studied and has been watching for a long time. He buys the stocks outright and then forgets them and goes back to baking. He may hold these stocks for three or four years, but when he sells them, he does so with substantial profits.

The most successful speculators are the fairly substantial business men whose daily work it is to keep in touch with business and credit conditions. These executives usually are sound and level-headed and often are familiar with the industries they are buying into.

CHARACTER AND STOCKS

Success or failure in the stock-market is largely a matter of the character of the speculator.

Luck and accident will cause temporary fluctuations of fortune in Wall Street, but in the end intelligence rules.

I have known many successful stock speculators, both large and small, and it has not been difficult to find the reason for their success. They had certain strongly marked characteristics that showed themselves in a few minutes of conversation.

Certain types may speculate with safety. Others

should shun the stock-market. The cold, unemotional, deliberate type of man or woman is likely to make the best speculator. The nervous, impulsive, unstable, and changeable person will have the least success.

There is one type that absolutely must not speculate, the credulous person who is a born dupe. Men and women of that type frequently are impatient and over-anxious and they are tortured by distorted imaginations.

People of the dupe type are hypnotized by the glare of gold. They stare so long at glistening fortune that their minds are brought under subjection to one of nature's strongest passions—greed. They will listen to any tip, however wild and ridiculous, and impulsively act on any suggestion.

The born dupe does not weigh facts, study conditions, or think of consequences. He sees only what he would like to possess and not what it is reasonably possible for him to obtain. He will borrow from friends, mortgage his home and furniture, borrow on insurance policies, and impoverish his family chasing phantoms that never could be real. This type never learns a lesson and will go on forever throwing good money after bad, waiting for his luck to turn. He gets in deeper and deeper with each transaction, and only stops when all his money is lost. There are hundreds of thousands of these dupes on the race-courses, in gambling-houses, and hanging around brokerage offices in Wall Street. You see them in the board rooms watching quotations with feverish faces and hungry eyes. They are often shrewd in certain lines of business and they would make more money attending to their own business.

A person must have cool judgment and a strong will to be a successful stock-market trader. Some other qualities he must have are: an accurate sense of values; caution; patience; suspicion; a mania for facts; courage; and the ability to withstand the charm of another's personality.

Where an individual intends to make stock speculation a profession, character is of even greater importance. There are three types of professional gamblers in the market, the bull, the bear, and the adjustable man who is part each.

The bear is a man who through some peculiar mental quirk absolutely cannot see the bright side of the business picture. He is always shaking his head over the awful calamities that are about to befall the stock-market and the nation. Stocks are always too high, in his opinion. Bears make huge profits quickly, but they lose them just as quickly.

The bull is a born optimist who never can see the top of the market. However high stocks go, he always believes they can go higher. He is always finding reasons for the market to go up. The sky is the limit, in his opinion. Both types come to grief because they do not know when to stop speculating. They are usually so blinded by their own prejudices that they do not watch out for danger signals. The bulls are more likely to be on the right side and pile up permanent fortunes, because this country is still growing, and in the ordinary course of evolution the industries of the United States must continue to expand. Expanding business means greater profits and higher returns for stockholders. High returns for stockholders mean higher stock prices. The bull is operating with growth. The bear makes his profits only at the expense of the mistakes of the bull.

The professional trader who is adjustable enough to be able to operate on both sides of the market is fortunate, but he has to be very clever and keep himself in perfect control.

Brokers are looking for customers, but they want intelligent customers. The few extra commissions made by the broker on the foolish trading of ignorant people do not compensate for the nasty and embarrassing situations that arise from such trading.

Many brokers learned to their sorrow in the crash of 1929 that it does not pay to give the unwise margin trader his head. Before accepting new accounts nowadays, brokers make some attempt to find out that the customer is responsible and knows what he is doing.

The speculator who foolishly throws his money away in the stock-market hurts himself, the broker, Wall Street, and the nation. Every surplus dollar by proper investment and wise speculation can be harnessed with other dollars to keep the country growing. The enormous waste of money in unwise speculation is unnecessary and a brake on the nation's prosperity.

WHAT IS INFORMATION?

Real information on stocks is not hard to find if you know where to look. The amateur speculator is misled and confused by a mass of misinformation masquerading under the guise of sound advice, but he does not take the trouble to check and double-check.

A speculator driven to desperation by his mistakes based on misinformation cried out to me: "Information? Where the devil is a man to turn to get accurate information?"

It is easy to tell a speculator to get accurate information, but where is he to get it? When he gets it, how is he to know that it is accurate?

The only information of use to the genuine speculator, not the trader, is basic information, and that can be obtained only at the source or from official quarters.

Accompanying this book will be found the names of certain official and private sources of information that can be relied upon. The public and private institutions mentioned will not give tips. They give information and the latest statistics obtainable. The speculator must decide for himself, after obtaining this information, what he wants to do in the market.

Accurate, unbiased information rarely comes to your door in the form of circulars or market letters. Statements made in such printed matter should be carefully checked by wise speculators. As a rule, the speculator has to seek information. It does not come to him.

There are plenty of outcast crooked firms in Wall Street who deliberately mislead the public with evasions and misleading statements in lurid circulars. These circulars just about get by the postal law and no more.

On the other hand, the reputable brokers send out daily and weekly market letters that are written honestly and conscientiously, but which also should be carefully checked.

Each brokerage house maintains a statistical department and has one man whose job it is to answer inquiry from customers by wire or over the telephone. This man does his work to the best of his ability, but he cannot know everything about all the stocks listed on the New York Stock Exchange and the New York Curb Exchange.

He is forced to rely upon the manuals of the various statistical organizations for his information or upon current gossip. The manuals are usually about one year old and many things may have happened since they were printed. Current gossip is a poor thing to base market operations on.

The information man in a brokerage house tries to protect himself and his customer. He cannot afford to make definite recommendations on stocks. He usually stays on the fence, and the substance of his advice is: "If stocks don't go up, they will go down." This is an obvious piece of advice, of little use to the man seeking a safe speculation.

Market-letter writers are usually picked for their knowledge of current stock market conditions and their ability to write rather than because of their knowledge of economics and business trends. But, however, there are a few who combine good stock market judgment with a study of broader trends.

The market-letter writer sits in his office ready to answer all questions on all stocks at a minute's notice. It can't be done. When he is stuck for an answer, he usually will say solemnly: "I think well of it" or "I think it is good for a long pull." This lets him out, but it does not help you.

The only conclusion worth anything in the market is that which you arrive at yourself after thorough investigation of basic facts. I know one man who deals in ten-share lots who would not think of buying a stock of any corporation until he has taken the trouble to seek interviews with the officers of the corporation whose stock he contemplates buying. Needless to say, this man has been very successful in a small way.

Important professional operators are not careless. They maintain large statistical organizations, which are constantly gathering data and analyzing business.

An experienced operator does not begin work in a stock until he knows all there is to know about it. He tries to figure the value to a penny. He knows just what he should pay for it, and what he must receive to show a profit.

Some amateur speculators also are wise.

One successful business man had about a million dollars to invest. Going to a large statistical organization, he asked them to compile a report for him showing the five most rapidly growing industries in the country. He asked the agency to pick out the leading companies in each of the five industries whose shares were listed on the Stock Exchange.

The business man paid a good fee for the report, but he was handsomely rewarded for his wisdom and forethought. His investment of a million dollars turned into many millions.

Here is a lesson for the smaller speculators whose thousands mean as much as the other man's millions. Accurate information on corporations is not difficult to get. The stock exchanges have on file data on all the stocks listed which is open to all.

Several reliable concerns in New York City make a business of gathering financial, trade and corporate information. These concerns make complete reports for a fee.

TIPS

One of the biggest operators in Wall Street once said to me: "When I want to sell stock, I make a point of buying that same stock publicly, or in a brokerage house where I know my operations will gain wide publicity."

This should be warning enough to amateur speculators to be slow in taking tips.

There is such a thing as a good tip, but it is very rare and it takes time to materialize. Few speculators want to wait a long time for a tip to make good.

Unless it comes true in a few days or a few months, they are disappointed and sell out.

A speculator should realize that he is not the first to hear the tip, but one of ten thousand. Even if the tip were good at the start, it is old before the average man hears it.

Information is the most valuable commodity in Wall Street. It is not given away. The moment news becomes public property, there is a reason. The information that really counts is the secret of a handful of men and they don't talk.

Tips are the bait used to catch credulous speculators. Some tips make good, but the speculators themselves, by their buying, usually make them come true.

A tip gathers power as it rolls along. Starting in Wall Street, it spreads over the country. The man who hears it last is the most likely to be left out on the highest limb of the tree.

A Wall Street professional interested in spreading a tip has no sentiment. He would pass it to his best friend if he thought it would gain wide circulation that way. The best way to start a tip working is to tell somebody and swear him to secrecy. The confidential aspect of the tip makes it all the more alluring.

The average tip-carrier likes to feel important. He invariably will distort the original information to make it look more interesting. No tipster is honest enough to say that he picked the gossip up in an unknown, unreliable place. Tip-carriers have nothing to go on except that somebody equally uninformed told them the story.

Some men have a mania for carrying tips on the stock-market just as others have a passion for whispering the names of horses that are bound to win.

The information is often spread around Wall Street that so-and-so (a big operator) is buying. He may be buying through one house and selling through half a dozen others. Big operators cover their tracks very carefully, because they know they have a following in the market.

It is wise to shun all tips.

Most tips purport to be inside information. Use your common sense and ask how an ordinary business acquaintance, the stranger you meet at a party, the manager of your hotel, or your barber could be in possession of inside information.

Even your broker who calls you on the telephone with a tip is taking a long chance. He picked the tip up from a newspaper man, another broker, or from the Wall Street grape-vine system. He knows nothing definitely. If he called you on the telephone, he has called a score of others.

Servants working for wealthy Wall Street men are great tip-carriers. A chauffeur, driving with immovable face, has both ears open if he knows he has anybody of importance in his car. An important Wall Street man has only to say he likes a certain stock within the hearing of one of the servants for the news to be spread immediately that Mr.

X. is buying the stock and that it is in for a big move.

Order-clerks in brokerage houses get excited if they see a big operator buying certain stocks. They immediately spread the news. This perhaps is just what the big operator wants. He may want to start public buying so that he can unload stock. It is ruinous to base stock-market operations on information such as this.

I have been a Wall Street writer for years and I know that certain interests tell me things in the hope that I will spread the news.

I also know that because I am a Wall Street writer most people would follow my advice in the market without question. In my own social circle, on the train, at affairs, the first thing people ask of me is a "tip on the market." This is true of all the other financial newspaper men. As a matter of fact, a Wall Street writer is constantly working to sift the real information from the propaganda.

Beware of the typical good-looking "wise guy" who calls big men by their first names. It is a hundred to one that he is a tip-carrier of the most virulent character.

LET THE BUYER BEWARE

Stocks are made to sell.

Let the buyer beware.

The motive behind all the churning round in the stock-market is the distribution of stock to the public by professional Wall Street.

There is nothing reprehensible about this. It is Wall Street's business to manufacture stock and to sell it. The ultimate consumers are the speculators and investors.

Wall Street is always on the selling side except when the speculative excesses of the public drive stocks down to bargain-counter prices. Then Wall Street is on the buying side. There are always plenty of professionals in the Street waiting to buy a dollar for seventy-five cents. But stock bought at bargain prices in the Street is only held against the time it can be resold to the public at a premium.

In Wall Street stock is a commodity to be sold at a quick profit. The manufacturers of stock want a quick turnover on their capital, as do the manufacturers of any other commodity.

Stock is sold by corporations in need of capital. The bankers who underwrite it and resell it to the public are interested only in performing their legitimate function as distributors.

The only way the speculator can beat the game is in buying good stocks and holding them until conditions warrant higher prices than he paid.

In order to attract buyers to its shop Wall Street has to do a great deal of window dressing, through publicity, of which some is legitimate and some is not. When the stock exchanges discover practices not strictly ethical, they are quick to punish the culprit. The exchanges and the banks spend large sums annually to catch crooks and to instruct the public in proper market procedure. But there is nobody to follow the unsophisticated round to keep him out of trouble.

The amateur speculator must use his head.

Stocks rarely get active unless somebody pulls the strings. The strings are pulled because there is stock for sale. The amateur speculator must realize that he is the ultimate goal of the person or persons behind the scenes. Large amounts of stock are distributed to the public by clever manipulation.

The speculator has nothing to fear if he chooses his stock carefully and has some idea of its intrinsic value.

Stocks being actively traded in day by day are in various stages of evolution. The stages are as follows:

1. Stocks that have arrived. These are called standard stocks. They are issued by the largest and best-managed corporations in the country and have been known to the public for periods of from five to twenty years. They have passed through all the agonies of birth and growth and usually are on a settled dividend basis. Elsewhere in this book will be found a partial list of standard stocks listed on the New York Stock Exchange. Any one of these stocks can be safely purchased by small speculators with the assurance that they will be worth more at some future date.

2. Second-grade stocks that have not quite reached the investment class. These are shares of newer corporations that are not old enough to have demonstrated their power to withstand all conditions and competition. These corporations may not have definitely established their positions in their particular fields of industry. Their earnings year by year may have been irregular and their dividends, if any are paid, may not be absolutely sure.

3. Stocks that are frankly new and unseasoned. Speculators as yet have not been able to arrive at any true estimate of their worth. It takes many years for stocks in this class to prove themselves.

4. Stocks of corporations that for one reason or another have gone downhill, with little or no hope of their ever recovering their lost positions.

5. Stocks that are absolutely worthless. Either they are manufactured for the sole purpose of swindling the public or they represent the dreams of a foolish visionary. Perhaps the man issuing such stocks thought he knew where he could find gold or oil and he wanted the public to finance the search. These stocks could not pass the listing requirements of any regular stock exchange.

This is an age of big business.

Almost every industry is controlled by large units, mostly the result of mergers of smaller units which were unable to fight competition.

Why risk your money financing the smaller units when shares of the controlling corporations can be purchased at about the same prices?

It is safer for small speculators to deal only in the shares of the larger, well-known corporations whose positions in industry are assured and whose dividend records have been steady and consistent.

If a speculator pays a little too much for shares in this class, he is not hurt, because he only has to hold them for a while and he will see a profit in the ordinary course of business development.

Beware of the shares of companies whose business is seasonal or depends on fads or fashions. These shares will fluctuate widely in price. In boom times they will be high, and in slack times they will drop out of sight.

The small speculator should keep away from all stock sold to finance novelties or experiments. Even perfectly good inventions in their early stages are not fit investments for the small speculator. The financing of such is the business of wealthy men.

A man walked into the office of a brokerage friend of mine with two hundred shares of stock in one of the earlier radio companies and asked if they had any value. He bought the stock in 1906 at ten dollars a share. The broker was unable to find the name of the concern in any records, and, of course, the stock had no value. This speculator had two thousand dollars tied up for more than twenty years, bringing in no income, and in the end he lost his principal.

In 1906 United States Steel common could have been bought for about eight dollars a share.

It must be remembered that Steel common in those days was on the suspicious list. Wall Street speculators did not believe that the corporation could survive. But the speculator mentioned would have been taking less chance buying into an industry like the steel industry than into a new and untried invention like radio. The radio industry now has arrived, but most of the early speculators who financed it lost their money, and even their names have been forgotten.

A new industry is built on the bones of thousands of speculators whose vision exceeded their financial powers and their common sense.

It is a good idea constantly to check investments and speculative holdings to see that they keep pace with the times. Gilt-edged investments of twenty years ago are some of the "cats and dogs" of today. This may be the fate of some of the modern first-class securities. Fashions in securities are constantly changing. New inventions, competition, shifts in population, any number of developments may change the fate of corporations.

Eternal vigilance is the price of safety in the stock-market. Speculators must keep abreast of the times and study the news carefully from day to day. With the generous space given to financial news in all the large daily newspapers, there is no excuse for ignorance.

THE MYSTERIOUS POOL

The whisper goes around the Street: "The pool is buying" or "The pool is selling" a certain stock, and speculators look wise and rush in to follow this mysterious force they know nothing about.

Following pool operations is a dangerous practice because the sole aim of most pools is to make stocks attractive to buyers at fictitious prices.

Pools represent organized speculation and manipulation and their sole aim is to unload stock on the public. While pools are careful not to break any of the by-laws of the Stock Exchange, their operations represent professional Wall Street at its worst.

While a pool is buying stock, it will do all in its power to encourage selling; and when it wants to resell to the public, it will go to great lengths to attract buyers. Some pools are thoroughly dishonest and will not hesitate to circulate false rumors and to manufacture news. Most of the false tips are deliberately circulated by pool managers.

A pool is a combination of men with capital who use their joint resources in a market operation in the belief that they can control the price by their buying and selling of a stock or group of stocks.

Sometimes there is a flimsy excuse for the formation of a pool. Its members may be in possession of advance knowledge of developments pending in the affairs of a certain corporation that will make its stock worth more or less.

Should a pool know of coming favorable developments, it will first try to depress the stock to buy it at low prices. Then when the good news comes out and the stock has a natural advance, it will sell out to the public.

If the news to come is unfavorable, the pool will try to boost the stock to high prices to unload and then go short of it.   In both cases the uninformed speculator is the victim. Either he is discouraged and shaken out of a good stock it would be profitable to hold, or he is lured into the market to buy stock that is riding for a fall.

The operations of a pool, all carried out under cover, are deceptive and treacherous even if they are not actually dishonest. Pool managers take advantage of ignorant speculators.

Pools usually are very cleverly organized and handled. Their managers make a thorough study of the stock they intend to operate in and never shoot in the dark. Before placing orders to buy or sell they have figured out almost to a penny the value of the stock in certain circumstances. They establish a maximum price they will pay for stock, and they will resort to various devices to obtain stock at or under that price.

A careful check-up is made by the pool of the whereabouts of every share of stock of the corporation involved. With the aid of stockholders' lists, easily obtainable, they know how much stock is in strong hands and how much is in weak hands. They know what stock is likely to come out of strong-boxes in case of a rise and what stock will not come to market. Then the amount of stock floating in Wall Street is ascertained.

If after all these carefully laid plans unexpected stock does come to market, the pool will back away until it has discovered where the stock is coming from. If the selling is from an important source, the operation may be dropped. If it is unimportant, the pool will let the stock decline until all the shares offered have been absorbed at low prices.

So well do most pool managers know the whereabouts of various blocks of stock that they can detect in a minute any unexpected offerings. It takes little time for them to trace the source of a sale.

If a pool plans to advance a stock five points, it will circulate the rumor that the stock is going to rise fifteen or even twenty points. The unsuspicious speculator holding for the fifteen points finds that the pool is through with its operation and he is left high and dry.

Sometimes pools make mistakes. They become over-ambitious or too optimistic or perhaps they become careless. Then their work in the market collapses, carrying with it scores of unwary speculators.

The only way to make money in a stock manipulated by a pool is to have accurate knowledge of when the pool is accumulating stock and what price it intends to sell at. It is almost impossible to obtain this information, because the success of a pool depends on its secrecy.

Even supposing that a speculator could learn the plans of a pool, there is still another danger, the sinister double cross. Men who lend themselves to pool operations will not hesitate if necessity arises to betray their friends.

Members of a pool usually sign an agreement not to sell their portion of the accumulated stock until a specified time, when all the members intend to sell. It is a common thing for one member of a pool to sell out if he can do it without being caught.

The honest pool is the buying group sometimes formed by bankers to protect a newly issued stock. Without some support in the market the new-comer might become a target for bear raids. This form of pool usually stands ready to take back all stock offered within a certain price range. The stock is then said to be "pegged." A buying pool of this character stays in existence until the new stock becomes seasoned and enjoys an active market without artificial support.

BE A BAD LOSER

Certain types of people would rather lose money in Wall Street and be able to brag about it than not speculate at all. They like to boast that they are "in the market."

Traders of this sort regard speculation as a game. When they lose, they are proud of it. "I had a good profit, but was taken to the cleaners," they tell their friends, and end with: "But I'm a good sport and know how to take my licking."

There is nothing to be proud of in taking losses. Speculation is not a game. It is the dead earnest business of making money. One should not speculate to show friends how well one can take a licking.

If being a "sport" means regarding philosophically all the opportunities missed, or not talking too much about winnings or losses, it is an asset. But if it means thinking too lightly of losses, or being too ready to take a loss, then it is a liability.

SENTIMENTALITY AND STOCKS

Sentimentality and stocks don't mix. A sentimental person is likely to place too much trust in a friend or relative. He will be certain that Mr. X would not give him a bad tip "because he is such a nice chap" or "because he knew my mother."

That you know a man socially or went to school with him is no reason to act on every suggestion he gives you concerning the stock-market.

THE BOARD FLY

It is unhealthy for the outside speculator to hang round Wall Street. There are too many temptations to buy and sell. Once having given his order, the speculator should go back to work and forget the market. He should not encourage his broker to telephone him every time the market changes. These scraps of information unsettle the mind and cause doubts.

Even the strongest-minded professionals are not proof against the tips and advice constantly circulating in Wall Street.

Standing round the board room of a brokerage house watching the fascinating little figures on the stock board or the movie ticker is dangerous. It seems such a pity not to take advantage of the daily swings in prices. Some people believe they can make a weekly salary catching those swings. They never do it.

Don't be tempted to take a flyer. It is in taking his first flyer that the new speculator gets hooked.

Board-room philosophy such as "Limit your losses and let your gains run on" is confusing. It sounds pretty, but in trying to limit your losses you dribble away money in a hundred transactions. Either you are in a good stock worth holding in which case don't worry, or your stock is on the suspicious list and you should not have bought it.

Another piece of Wall Street philosophy is "You never go broke taking a profit." This cannot be denied, but it is calculated to turn you into an active trader. To take quick profits you must be constantly jumping in and out of the market. You want substantial and safe profits, and you don't care how long you wait for them.

A few old traders in the Street try to teach the science of tape-reading. This is a lost art. The market is too big and broad now to judge a stock by its action on the tape. Chart-reading was a high art in the days before the war, when only a handful of stocks were traded in and a million-share day was a record. Charts are of doubtful value to the speculator today.

Don't talk too much about the market to your friends. You will attract too many opinions and too much of the "They say" type of information.

JOINT ACCOUNT

Don't be persuaded to open a joint account in the stock-market with another person. Even in business partners rarely agree; in the stock-market they never do.

Always at the crucial moment one partner wants to do one thing, and the other partner something different. When you want to sell the stock owned jointly, the other fellow wants to hold it, and so it goes on. Where there is a difference of opinion, somebody is wrong, and should money be lost because of wrong judgment, there is bitterness and wrangling.

Only one person can run an account in the stock-market. Then the glory or responsibility is properly placed and there is no room for argument. Two persons very rarely agree as to the time to buy or sell stocks.

I recall two friends who opened a joint account some years ago, each putting five hundred dollars into the pool. They fought and wrangled for almost a year and showed profits of about two thousand dollars. Then came the break, the men parted, and the profits were split. One man took his fifteen hundred dollars and ran it up into a fortune. He later became a member of a Stock Exchange firm. The other fellow continued to speculate in his own way, but was not so successful. If you are superstitious, you probably believe that the luck of two people does not run the same way, and that only disaster can follow the crossing of luck.

THE DISCRETIONARY ACCOUNT

It is a common practice, and a most unsatisfactory one, for an amateur speculator to give a man at the broker's office, or a professional trader, discretionary powers over his account. The speculator, ignorant of the market, opens a trading account in a brokerage house and empowers somebody to speculate for him.

This system rarely works out in favor of the speculator. Either the man handling the account is too timid to do any good with his client's money or he is too bold because he has nothing to lose by his mistakes.

The trader who lets somebody else speculate with his money is taking great chances of meeting dishonesty. In an active market the agent could make many trades that the trader knew nothing about.

My first and last experience with a discretionary account came shortly after I started speculating. I opened a small account in a small brokerage house and empowered one of the customers' men to do my trading for me. I soon found that when the trade was successful, I never heard of it. When it was unsuccessful, it went into my account. This man was later discharged for dishonesty. The Stock Exchange looks with disfavor on its members' accepting discretionary accounts.

OPENING A BROKERAGE ACCOUNT

When you decide to open an account in the market, be sure you pick a good broker. You don't want to wake up one morning and read that your broker has gone into receivership with liabilities greatly exceeding assets.

The surest check you have on a broker is to find out whether he is a member of a regular exchange. A call or a letter to the secretary of the exchange will bring this information. Strict rules govern the members of all the large exchanges, and the governing bodies make periodical investigations of the members' financial position.

There are good brokers not members of exchanges, but extra care must be used in checking their reputations. There are numerous ways of checking an independent broker. One way is to ask your local banker what he knows about him. Another is to write to one of the large Wall Street banks for information. The Better Business Bureau would give a quick answer. There are certain agencies that will furnish confidential credit ratings on anybody for a fee. All good newspapers check their financial advertising carefully and make an investigation of all advertisers.

The client on his side is asked to establish his financial position and his right to trade before an account will be accepted by any good broker. The broker wants to know that you will honestly come to the protection of your account should occasion arise.

Under the rules of the Exchange the broker must deny the privilege of trading to employees of banks, trust companies, insurance companies, and stock-exchange firms unless the written permission of the employer has been obtained.

Should you want to buy stock outright for cash, you simply place your order and give the broker a check. When the stock is delivered to you, the transaction is closed.

A margin account is open as long as the customer desires it. The client is required to maintain a margin with the broker at all times sufficient to carry the securities bought for him. This margin is a matter of arrangement between the customer and the broker. The size of the margin will depend on current credit and market conditions and the type of stock to be bought.

In the middle of big speculative movements the broker will ask for a higher margin of protection than during dull markets. He will want a higher margin on the more volatile speculative stocks than he would demand on the good standard stocks that do not fluctuate so widely.

Be advised by your broker on the amount of stock to buy. He knows when you are in the danger zone. Don't argue with him about letting you buy more stock than in his judgment you should. Almost the first question put to the broker by a new margin trader is: "How much can I buy on this?" Invariably the new trader will buy up to the hilt.

Every purchase or sale of securities for a client by a member of one of the large exchanges is a *bona fide* purchase or sale and involves the disbursement or receipt of cash and actual receipt and delivery of securities. In a bucket-shop these transactions are just book-keeping entries.

On opening a margin account you must put up either cash or good securities that can be used by the broker as collateral for a loan at the bank. The amount your broker will allow you on your securities is governed by the amount his banker will lend him on the collateral. Changes in market conditions affect the value of the securities behind the loan.

In buying and selling securities you probably will do business either personally or over the telephone with a "floor man" or "customers' man" at the broker's office. Form your own opinion of his ability to advise you safely and act accordingly. Don't think that you are compelled to act on his advice.

In giving orders you must be specific, giving the name of the stock, the time when you want to buy or sell it, and the price. Don't leave anything to chance or take anything for granted. Remember money is involved.

You must tell your broker whether you want to buy or sell "at the market" or at a certain price. These terms are explained in the financial dictionary accompanying this book.

Orders given "at the market" are unrestricted as

to price and are subject to immediate execution at the best price obtainable. It is the broker's duty to the customer to execute the order on the most favorable terms.

Don't be surprised if your order is executed at considerably higher or lower prices than you expected. In active markets the stock ticker may be from ten minutes to an hour behind the market, and prices on the floor of the exchange where the order is to be executed may be much higher or lower than prices on the ticker. That the stock you want to buy or sell was quoted at one hundred when you looked at it last on the ticker is no reason why it should be at that price when the order is executed. The order may be executed anywhere from one to twenty points away from the ticker price. It is a good idea to ask the broker for a "bid and asked" price before giving an order. That is the very latest quotation from the floor. In ordinary markets the broker will execute your order in a few minutes and report the price back to you. In very active markets, when there is a congestion of orders, it will take longer to get a report.

The margin trader should familiarize himself with the various Wall Street terms used in buying and selling stock.

The customer may want to buy or sell stock otherwise than at the market. He may, for instance, believe a decline is due in the market, and that if he waits, he will buy his stock lower, or he may believe an advance is due and put his selling order in above current levels.

It is possible to put orders in the broker's hands that are automatically executed. These are called "open orders." An open order is good until executed by the broker or cancelled by the customer. An open order may be specified "good for a week" or "good for a month." Unless otherwise specified, all open orders are considered by the broker to be for the day only. An open order is executed immediately the stock reaches the price specified by the customer provided other orders at that price have not been entered ahead.

The customer, if he changes his mind about buying or selling the stock, must remember to cancel the open order immediately.

A common form of order specifying the conditions under which stock is to be sold is a "stop loss order." A stop loss order usually is placed below or above current prices according to whether the trader is long or short to limit loss or to insure paper profits. Active professional traders on the buying side will follow an advancing stock with stop loss orders just under the selling price to "cinch" their profits in case of a sudden turn in the market.

Traders who are gambling in a dangerous market, which might turn about at any moment, place a stop loss order at a price several points below the current selling price, or at a price beyond which they cannot afford to lose.

A stop loss order to buy or sell becomes a "market order" when the stock sells "at or above" or "at or below" the stop price. The decline or advance in the market is accelerated in waves as layer after layer of stop loss orders are uncovered. In a declining market bear traders do their best to depress prices to a point where large volumes of stop loss orders will automatically be executed.

The execution of these orders is in a measure forced selling. In an advancing market the shorts will have stop loss orders above current prices, and bull traders will fight to force prices up to a point where these stop loss orders will be caught. This is in the nature of forced covering and greatly accelerates the upward pace of the market.

The customer usually receives a notice of the execution of his order in the mail the day following execution of the trade. The notice will show the price paid for the stock, the commission charged by the broker, and the taxes collected by the Government on the sale of the stock.

Once a month the broker will render the customer a statement showing in detail the purchases and sales of the month. The statement will show the interest and charges made by the broker for carrying the stock on margin. Minimum rates of commission charged by the broker are fixed by the exchange, and no broker is allowed to deviate from those rates. Taxes are collected by the Federal Government on each share of stock sold, and some of the states collect taxes. In putting the tax on your bill the broker is simply collecting it for the Government. Taxes are paid by the seller.

The broker charges you interest for the time he is supplying you with funds to carry on your operations. If in your collateral you have interest-bearing securities, the broker will credit your account with the interest as received. If in your margin account you have dividend-bearing stock, the broker will credit your account with the dividends as collected. Should any "rights" accrue to the customer on stock he is carrying, the broker will take care of the subscription on orders from the customer.

STOCK DELIVERY

Under the rules of the Stock Exchange all settlements of transactions are made the next full business day. In other words, stock bought today must be delivered and paid for tomorrow. This enormous amount of work is handled through the Stock Clearing Corporation.

Stock is not delivered to the margin trader unless he asks for it and pays for it. The stock bought by the margin trader is kept in the broker's loan account. The trader can demand it at any time at the price he paid for it if he wants to buy the stock outright and put it away.

When a seller fails to deliver a security within a reasonable time, the purchaser may demand immediate delivery. If this demand is not complied with, the purchaser may buy the security on the Exchange at prevailing prices, and any difference in price must be paid by the seller. This is called "buying in."

ODD LOTS

If you are a ten-share trader don't be ashamed of it.

Odd lots—that is, buying in amounts less than a round lot of a hundred shares—constitute a large part of the daily business on the Stock Exchange.

Three large houses in the Street act as dealers in odd lots buying from and selling to other brokerage houses. They maintain a large corps of brokers on the floor of the Stock Exchange.

At times odd-lot buying by hundreds of thousands of small traders has been powerful in swinging the market against the larger traders.

Many of the biggest traders today started their Wall Street careers buying odd lots.

It is better to buy stock in odd lots and be able to protect your margin than to attempt to look big in buying hundred-share lots and not be able to protect your account.

If you learn to creep with odd lots, you may be able to fly some day with a much larger account. If you overbuy at the start, you will cripple yourself financially.

An odd-lot order given to your broker is subject to the same rules that govern a thousand-share order except that the odd-lot trader has to pay an eighth or a quarter of a point more for his stock than the buyer of a round lot. Your broker will pass the odd-lot order on to an odd-lot house for execution.

After the odd-lot order leaves the customer's hands, it is given to an order-clerk in the office of the commission house in which he is doing business. The order is then telephoned to the firm's telephone clerk on the floor of the Stock Exchange, who writes it out, stamps on it the name of the odd-lot dealer who handles the firm's old-lot business, and gives it to an employee of the Stock Exchange in charge of a sending station of the pneumatic-tube system.

The order goes to the particular post where the stock is listed. There it is given to the odd-lot dealer or put on the hook assigned to him. Its treatment then depends on whether it is a market order, a limited order, or a stop order. If the order is a market order to buy, the odd-lot dealer reports it at a price an eighth or a quarter above the first price of a round lot of that particular stock that is quoted after the order is in his hands; or, if it is a sell order, an eighth or a quarter below.

Limited orders are executed at their limits except where the first sale of a round lot after receipt of the order permits of its execution at a price better than the limit. Stop orders are executed at an eighth to a quarter from the sale that puts the stop order in force.

An odd-lot customer who does not want to wait for a sale to occur to have his order executed can in the case of "quarter" stocks sell or buy an eighth away from the bid or offered price, and in the case of "eighth" stocks at the bid or offered price.

An order to sell or buy an odd lot at the close of the market will be executed at the bid or offered price and not at the price of the last sale.

This sounds like a very complicated process, but such is the efficiency of the odd-lot houses that an order under a hundred shares is executed with the same speed that is used in the execution of a round lot.

Odd lots are handled by odd-lot dealers on the following terms: All stocks selling at 99⅞ and under, at one-eighth from the sale or on the bid and offer, and all stocks selling at 100 and over, one-fourth from the sale or at one-eighth from the bid and offer.

WELL BOUGHT IS HALF SOLD

Speculators as a rule pay too much for their stock in the first place. In the words of Wall Street, they have a poor "market position."

The average venture into the Street in search of profits usually resolves itself into a long-drawn-out fight to get out of the market with a whole skin.

At this minute there are hundreds of thousands of speculators praying for stocks to return to the prices they paid for them. It is a good bet that these unfortunate traders never will wait for that time, but will sell at a loss.

It is an equally good bet that the market will not advance far enough for these traders to sell at a profit while it knows of the overhanging weak stock.

It is not in the nature of professional Wall Street to climb for stocks or to pay fancy prices for them. Wall Street will buy at its own price, and that price has to be at or below the actual value of the stock.

The pools and professional operators go to a lot of trouble loading the public with stock at inflated prices. They are not disposed to take the stock back at those prices. The only chance one "lamb" has to get out even or better is to find another "lamb" to sell to. This might happen in a rampant bull market when large numbers of tyros are in the market buying anything in sight at any price.

A man who goes into the market in search of a quick profit and gets hooked with a quick loss is known as an "involuntary investor." He is not investing in a stock because he wants to hold it, but because, once having paid top price for it, he can't get out without a loss.

The novices in Wall Street are always buying at the top and getting sold out at the bottom. Cynical professional traders say: "The Street [meaning the rank and file of speculators who fill the commission houses] is always wrong."

One well-known plunger said he made his fortune by doing exactly the opposite in the market "of what everybody else was doing."

The stock-market is most dangerous when it looks the best. When stocks are making sensational advances, it means that pools are throwing out smoke-screens to cover their selling, and that the "lambs" are tumbling over one another in an effort to swallow the bait and hook. This is the time to sell, not to buy.

The time to buy is when everything looks black and nobody wants stocks. Then the trader can buy at his own price.

Buying should not be done in a hurry. There is usually plenty of time to buy good stocks. If there seems to be need for haste, the time is not ripe for bargain-hunting.

The market moves up slowly, but it goes down fast. In the crash of 1929 a year's advance was wiped out in about two weeks.

The stock-market actually is a barometer of business, credit, and world affairs. It moves in cycles covering periods of three years or more. But sometimes the working of these cycles is halted temporarily by speculation based on current happenings. It is not always easy to discern whether it is a bull or a bear market.

Prices move up and down in wide swings over long periods, but between these extreme points there will be many shorter swings, or the market will move sideways.

The market never moves steadily one way. It does not advance over a long period without a set-back now and again, and it does not decline without periodical rallies.

The set-backs or reactions in bull markets occur when the market becomes "over-bought" at high prices. This is the signal for the bears to begin raiding. The temporary rallies in bear markets are caused when the market becomes "oversold." Then the bear traders whose selling helped bring about the decline rush to cover, and bull traders buy for a "quick turn."

The wise speculator who buys for the "long pull" or to catch the major swings pays no heed to the temporary conditions described. He bought his stock at a low price originally and he intends holding it for a long time until his profit is substantial enough to take.

All the deflation in values in the stock-market in the fall of 1929 never endangered properly invested capital. Good stocks declined with the bad during the break, but when the pressure was relieved, the good stocks snapped right back.

Traders who carried more good stocks than they could afford to buy had to suffer with the speculators who were loaded up with poor issues. This was the penalty they paid for "over-extension." Buying too much stock is the cardinal sin in Wall Street.

Unless a speculator was forced to sell to lighten his margin account, he was not hurt in the break. Those speculators who knew the rules of Wall Street and held good stocks that they could buy outright if necessary sat back and watched events as interested spectators.

No matter how good a stock is, it is certain to fluctuate in price. These minor fluctuations mean nothing. The only factors that could make a corporation's stock worth more, such as increased business, expansion of operations, increased earnings, changes of management, and developments of major importance, don't happen overnight nor every day of the week.

Only over long periods can a stock be expected to really increase in intrinsic worth. It is not common sense to believe that a stock could be worth, say, $100 today and $125 tomorrow. These fluctuations are caused by pool manipulation and public speculation and should not interest the speculator who has bought intelligently. All buying in the stock-market must be done on an intelligent plan and according to rules.

The man who pursues one policy one day and another the next is going to run into trouble.

A horde of unintelligent speculators plunge into the market without forethought and without plans. They operate blindly and blame Wall Street for their own mistakes. They are buying when the professionals are selling, and selling when Wall Street is buying.

The stock exchanges cannot be blamed for the woes of speculators. They don't approve or disapprove of speculation. They simply provide a convenient meeting-place for people who want to buy and sell stock.

A story is told of a man who wanted to be constantly in the market and asked his brokers to tip him off on anything good. One day the Federal Reserve Bank rediscount rate was raised to five per cent. The broker sent a telegram to his customer:

"Bank rate up five."   Back came a telegram from the customer: "Buy me a thousand shares."

This is how numerous speculators operate and the foolish, reckless policy was responsible for losses of approximately four billion dollars in the great 1929 crash. People suffered the agony of financial loss and many had to start life over again because they would not take the trouble to learn the rules of the game they were playing.

It is not easy to know when to buy stock. The daily fluctuation of prices is confusing, destroying true values. It is not easy even for professional Wall Street to figure the exact value of a stock. There are many intangible elements to be reckoned with.

The purchaser of common stock becomes a partner in the corporation, and he shares in the success or failure of the business. Often in the liquidation of a company there is nothing left for the common stockholders.

On the other hand, the common shares of many of the large corporations have large assets behind them and are immensely valuable. The size of the corporation, the nature of its business, its position in its particular line, the book value of the company's assets, the capitalization ahead of the common stock, the dividends paid, the company's present and future prospects, all have to be considered in figuring the value of common stock.

This problem is too intricate for the average trader, who must rely upon a good statistical agency to figure it out for him. It must be borne in mind that the stock has a true value, and somebody knows what that value is, regardless of market prices. Sometimes a rough idea of the value of a stock can be gained by a study of the high and low prices of the year and previous years, but rough estimates are not advisable.

It is impossible to pick the extreme low price or the extreme high price. If you come close to either of those points, you are clever.

The Japanese have a proverb which means that they are always satisfied with seventy-five per cent. This is a good proverb for small speculators to keep in mind. Nothing is gained by trying to gain a hundred per cent profit in the stock-market. Don't be greedy. When you have a satisfactory reward for your skill and patience, take your profit and be satisfied.

Many speculators hang on to their stocks too long, believing that if they can make twenty points, they can just as easily make a hundred. There is danger in waiting for the last eighth. When a stock becomes inflated, every point up increases the danger of a sudden break.

Traders sometimes make up their minds to sell at a certain point. When the stock reaches that point, everything looks so rosy that they decide to postpone selling. They usually overstay their market.

In buying stock make the investigation before the purchase and not after. The right time to buy is after a decline, but be sure the decline is over. After the first crash last fall, thousands of speculators rushed in to buy stocks, believing the storm had passed. This crop of buyers had the heaviest losses. The second crash was worse than the first.

After a bad smash the stock-market does not recover from the shock immediately. Sometimes it takes months to regain the vitality to move upward again.

These dull periods after declines are the ideal buying times, when bankers and large operators accumulate stocks.

When the market backs and fills at fairly stabilized levels after a crash, you are almost sure that it is scraping the bottom.

The time to buy is after a big decline or in the early stages of a bull market, but few of the smaller traders have the courage to do this. They feel safer following the crowd.

Before buying after a smash watch the market for a little while to be sure another storm is not brewing. If the market has hit the bottom, and stocks start to slowly rise again, you may have to pay a few points more for your stock by waiting, but you will be sure.

Generally a stock will find its correct level in the market. It may sell above its worth for a time or perhaps a little below, but in the end the market's estimate will be fairly accurate. The business of the speculator is to make a thorough study of the stock he intends to buy and by watching its market action decide for himself where the level of true worth is. Having decided this, let him wait patiently until the stock sells at his price before buying. It will get there in time.

New speculators believe that a stock that is quoted at a low price must be cheap. It may turn out to be very expensive. Stocks do not decline to low prices and stay there without a reason. If you notice a stock selling at very low figures now, whereas it used to sell at high prices, step warily. There may be a receivership or an assessment in the offing. On the other hand, a stock selling at a very high price is not always worth it.

The speculator is fairly safe if he makes an investigation of all the known facts concerning a stock, does not listen to tips, and does not act in a hurry. Professional traders give their own ideas about when a stock should be bought, but there is only one safe rule—buy it at or near its true worth.

It is just as difficult to know when to sell as when to buy. It is not advisable to look for quick profits, and it is not advisable to hold on too long. The speculator must be guided by intelligence and what he believes the stock to be worth.

If the trader has a fairly accurate knowledge of the value of stock when he buys, he must have some notion of what would be a fair price for him to sell at without expecting miracles to happen.

The speculator who bought when everybody was selling is pretty sure of a profit if he sells when everybody is buying. This is a very simple rule, but workable.

When a trader has broken the rules and purchased

pool stock at inflated prices, he should sell it as soon as he finds out his mistake. Better take a small loss immediately than hold on to second- or third-rate stocks for a long period, only to sell them in the end at a big loss.

It takes courage to take a loss deliberately, but it is the wise thing to do if you are wrong. Many traders get hooked in low-grade stocks at high prices and doggedly hold on to them in the vain hope that they will come back. The trader who would buy this class of stock undoubtedly has a limited margin, and he knows he will have to let go in the end. He might as well sell and save the broker's carrying-charges.

THE SCALPER

In his dangerous trade the "scalper" is satisfied with very small profits. After he has paid commissions, he finds his profits small indeed. The "scalper" is a nimble gentleman who sits huddled over the ticker all day and takes no lunch until after the market closes. A man who tries to be a "scalper" from his home or office, trusting to telephoned information from Wall Street, is doomed to failure.

The nimble speculators of that type provide an active market for stocks at all times. It is their differences of opinion that makes it possible for the legitimate investor or speculator to sell.

Don't try to outguess the market. It can't be done. About fifteen million people in this country are trading in stocks. Their buying and selling, mostly ill-advised, changes the market from day to day. You can't hope to gauge their hopes and fears.

THE CHRONIC TRADER

The chronic trader works himself into a buying frenzy. He must be buying, buying, buying. And consequently he is losing, losing, losing. His judgment, if he ever had any, becomes warped and his mind depressed. He gets into a pessimistic frame of mind and believes luck has deserted him. Each time he tries to get out of an old hole, he falls into a new one, and finally despairs. Now is the time for him to quit speculation for a while.

Every seasoned gambler knows the value of a positive frame of mind. The soul attracts what it most desires or fears. You must have the winning spirit in the stock-market.

Professional traders catch the buying fever too, only they know the symptoms. The moment they feel it coming on, they close their accounts and go away for a rest.

It is most essential that the stock trader keep from worrying. He can do this only if he is speculating wisely, buying good stocks (preferably dividend-paying) that have stood the test of time.

It is easy to fall into the bad habit of chronic trading. If you have a sudden stroke of good fortune, you believe you can duplicate it. If you have a piece of bad luck and lose money, you are over-anxious to make it up. You are then getting into a feverish state of mind.

Having sold your stock at a profit, keep it warm in the bank for a time while you think out a new plan. Don't get reckless and dash into the market again, or your profits will melt.

SHORT SELLING

As the market falls faster than it goes up, the bear makes quicker and larger profits than the bull, but he takes many more risks. When a bull trader buys a stock, he knows how far it can fall—no lower than zero. A bear trader who sells short, and must cover his commitment some day, does not know how far a stock can go up.

If he is unlucky enough to sell a closely held stock that is "cornered," he may have to cover at fantastic prices and suffer heavy losses. The bulls have many tricks to encourage the bears to sell stocks short with the idea of trapping them and running the market up on their covering operations.

Enormous fortunes have been made quickly on the short side of the market, but Wall Street history records few of them that were ever retained. The trader who feels he must have the experience of selling stock short had better make sure that he is selling a widely held stock that will be easy to buy back. If he is not careful, he will sell into a bag from which he cannot escape. Knowing the risks of the short side, brokers do not encourage amateur traders to operate on that side of the market. Leave short selling to the professionals.

A WORD ON STOCK SWINDLING

Hundreds of millions of dollars in worthless stock are sold each year by swindlers. This stock is never listed on any regular exchange, but is peddled over the telephone or from door to door.

Don't listen to sales talks of men who call on the telephone or ring the door-bell. Good securities don't go begging for buyers. The buyer has to go looking for them. High-pressure salesmen are successful only as long as they can keep prospective buyers from thinking. The purveyors of worthless stock base all their hopes of success in putting through whirlwind selling-campaigns.

Before buying stock of any kind, find out who is selling it and go to a lot of trouble investigating the firm.

Don't sign over your good securities to strangers who have only gold bricks to give you in return.

AVERAGING

The system of averaging to lower the cost price of a stock that has declined after the trader bought it is safe only under certain conditions.

Suppose a trader bought stock at a hundred dollars a share, and it declined to ninety dollars; he can lower his net cost and more quickly get into a profitable position by taking on additional stock at the lower price.

This practice is advisable only if the trader is certain that he has a good stock that was cheap when he bought it originally. Then the decline simply offers him a good opportunity to pick up a bargain. He must be sure that in taking on the additional stock he is not overloading his account.

If the stock purchased originally was of doubtful value, to buy more is to get deeper in the hole, particularly as there is no guarantee that the stock will not continue to decline.

SWITCHING

Many active traders who have taken a loss in a stock attempt to make it up immediately by switching into another stock that either is moving up or is expected to move. This practice is not for the wise speculator. It more often than not means jumping out of the frying-pan into the fire.

PAPER PROFITS

Don't spend your paper profits. A profit is not a profit until the trader has the cash in hand.

It is quite human, but very unsound, to figure up how much money you would have if you sold your stocks and to live accordingly. If something happens to the market, and your profits disappear as fast as they came, you are out the money you expected to have and the real cash you have spent in anticipation of taking the profits.

PYRAMIDING

The trader who pyramids his profits is undertaking one of the most speculative ventures in the market. This is done by purchasing additional stock on paper profits. The system is permitted by brokers, but the operator doing it is watched closely for margin.

Traders who pyramid must be absolutely certain that a big rise is due in the stock. They are building up a house of cards that could easily collapse. It is an "all or nothing" proposition, not recommended for the amateur trader.

Where to Go for Information

The New York Stock Exchange will send by return mail the listing application of any stock listed on the Exchange, giving complete information up to listing.

The New York Curb Exchange answers all inquiries from the public.

The Department of Commerce in Washington makes regular reports on business conditions, industry, and foreign trade.

The Federal Reserve Board and the Federal Reserve banks make public regular reports on business, industry, and credit conditions.

Banks in every town maintain statistical departments to assist their depositors in making wise investments.

The financial departments of the leading newspapers are glad to answer inquiries on stocks and bonds.

The Better Business Bureau in New York City and similar bureaus in other cities are ready to an-

swer all questions concerning doubtful stocks
or doubtful financial institutions. A call at their
offices will bring an 'mmediate check on a
broker or a stock.

Some well-known private statistical organizations:
   The Standard Statistics Company
   Harvard Economic Service
   Brookmire Economic Service, Inc.
   Moody's Investors' Service

Advice from the United States Steel Corporation

The following rules designed by George K. Leet, Secretary of the United States Steel Corporation, are enclosed with dividend checks sent to stockholders:

1. Keep your certificates in a safe place. A bureau drawer, trunk, or coat-pocket is not a safe place.

2. A surety bond is required before new certificates will be issued to replace those which have been lost. Bonds are expensive.

3. Do not sign your name on your stock certificates until you are ready to dispose of them. If you do, they may be transferred out of your name without your knowledge.

4. When considering the sale of certificates, consult a reputable banker, broker, or other competent person whose integrity cannot be questioned. Do not surrender them, for any reason, without careful investigation.

5. Keep a record of your certificates, their number, the number of shares, etc. It may be useful.

6. In forwarding certificates anywhere, for any purpose, it is well to do so by registered mail.

7. If your certificates are lost or stolen, please notify the corporation immediately; also if and when recovered.

8. Somebody has toiled and saved for the certificates you own. If kept, they will add to your comfort and independence in old age.

ACTIVE STOCK—Frequently dealt in and often appearing on the stock ticker tape.

ARBITRAGE—Buying and selling securities on different markets, taking advantage of temporary differences in price. For instance, buying in New York and selling in Montreal or London.

ASKED PRICE—The price at which the owner of a security is willing to sell.

ASSESS—Additional funds over what they paid for stock, asked by a corporation of its stockholders. Sometimes done to prevent bankruptcy.

ASSENTED—Referring to securities deposited under an agreement by which the owners agree to certain changes in a corporation's organization.

ASSETS—The possessions of a corporation. Quick assets are cash and securities readily turned into cash. Slow assets are plants, real estate, patents, etc.

ASSIGN—To transfer ownership in writing.

AT MARKET—An order given to a broker by a customer to buy or sell a stock immediately at the prevailing price.

AT OPENING—An order given to a broker to buy or sell when the market opens, or at the first quotation of a certain stock.

AVERAGING—Purchasing securities on a scale down after having made one purchase at a certain price. This is done to lower the average cost.

BALLOONING—Professional strong-arm methods to advance a stock to fictitious levels.

BEAR—A trader who believes the market is too high because of unfavorable conditions. Bear operators borrow stock to sell at prevailing prices, hoping to make a profit by purchasing later at a lower price.

BEAR MARKET—A declining market.

BEAR PANIC—A rapid recovery in prices due to short covering. The bears have been frightened into buying at a loss to make deliveries of stock already borrowed and sold.

BID PRICE—The price a buyer is willing to pay for a stock. There is often a sizable difference between the bid and asked price of stocks, and the transaction is mostly put through at a price at or close to the bid price.

BLIND POOL—A combination of men formed to put through certain market operations. The operation is conducted by an agent who has a free hand. His actions may not be known or understood by the other members of the pool.

BLOCK—A substantial number of shares or bonds bought or sold in one transaction.

BOILER SHOP—The telephone nest of a stock swindler. Here young men are trained in high-pressure selling methods. By dynamic talks on the telephone they are able to sell large amounts of worthless stock to people they have never seen.

BOND—A negotiable security payable at a fixed time and at a fixed rate of interest. A bond is usually secured by real estate, plants, or other securities valued at a greater price.

BONDED DEBT—The total amount of bonds a corporation has outstanding.

BOOKS CLOSE—In making a list of stockholders entitled to a dividend or vote at stockholders' meetings a corporation announces a certain date on which its transfer books will be closed.

BOOKS OPEN—Transfer books reopened after a meeting. Between the two dates stock cannot be transferred.

BOOK VALUE—The value placed by a corporation on its books of all its assets.

BORROWING STOCK—Traders who sell short have to borrow stock from somebody else. All stock sold must be delivered the next day. The broker who borrows the stock pays the market price for it. He has the privilege of returning it at the same price. The lender can demand the return of the stock at any time.

BORROWING AT A RATE—A stock that is scarce must be borrowed "flat." This means that the borrowing broker gets no interest on the money paid to the lender. Sometimes the borrower can obtain interest rates near the market. At times he has to pay a premium to borrow stock. In corners shorts have to pay exorbitant prices to borrow stock.

BOTTOM PRICES—The low point of a downward move.

BREAK—A sudden decline in prices.

BROKEN LOT—Less than a round lot of a hundred shares.

BUCKETING—The illegal practice of buying and selling stock on paper without any actual transaction. The broker sells or buys against his customers' orders.

BUCKET SHOP—A fake brokerage house where bucketing takes place. The business consists in placing bets on the rise and fall of prices. Bucketing usually is done in small amounts. Unsuspecting customers write out orders in the regular way, but they are never executed. There is no transfer or delivery of stock. The "Bucketeer" wants customers to trade on small margins so that they are wiped out on very small price swings in the market.

BULGE—A sudden unexpected advance in prices.

BULL CAMPAIGN—A well-planned effort by professional traders or bankers to put the market up.

BULL—One who believes prices should go higher and operates accordingly. A bull buys in the hope that he will be able to sell at a higher price. The constructive trader is called a bull because, like that animal, he tosses stocks higher. A bear got the name because he tears down with his claws. The bull and the bear are eternal enemies on the stock exchange and are always at war because they have opposite opinions.

BUYING IN—When a seller fails to deliver a security on time, the purchaser may demand immediate delivery. If delivery is not made, the purchaser may buy the security on the exchange at prevailing prices. The difference in price must be paid by the seller.

BUYER'S OPTION—The demand for delivery of certificates within a specified time, by the purchaser of a stock.

BUY OUTRIGHT—When full payment is made for stock at the time of purchase.

CALL—An option at a price to call on an individual for specified stock at a stated price within a stated period. The holder of a call does not have to exercise it. The buyer of a call usually believes the market is going higher. The seller of the call is gambling that the market will not go higher.

CALLABLE—The right of a corporation to redeem securities before the maturity date.

CALL LOAN—A loan to brokers by a bank or a money dealer payable on demand. Most of the business on the stock exchange is done with call loans.

CARRYING CHARGES—The interest and other charges made by the broker to carry stock on margin. This is over and above commission.

CASH SALE—Delivery of securities bought and paid for at once.

CLEARED—Of the clearing of money and securities among brokers at the end of the day.

CLOSE CORPORATION—A company whose shares are held by a few persons and rarely come to market for sale.

CLOSED OUT—This happens to a trader on margin who has failed to provide additional funds when asked to by the broker. The broker sells out the stock for what it will bring, without the consent of the customer.

COLLATERAL—Securities pledged with a broker instead of cash as margin against stock purchases. The broker allows only a percentage of the value of the collateral to be used in the speculative account.

COMMISSION—The charge made by a broker for buying and selling stock.

COMMON STOCK—The shares of a corporation upon which dividends may be paid only after the requirements of the bonds and preferred stock have been taken care of.

COMPARISONS—The comparing by stock exchange houses of transactions to correct errors.

CONTROLLING COMPANY—A corporation that through stock ownership and representation on directors' boards controls the affairs of other companies.

CONVERTIBLE BOND—One which can be exchanged for the stock of the same company at stated times and at stated prices.

COPPERS—A general term used to designate the group of shares of all the copper companies listed on the Exchange.

CORNER—Where a secretly organized combination of financial interests has bought up all the floating supply of shares of a certain company. With no stock offered and under the influence of urgent bids from the pool, there is no limit to the price a cornered stock may reach. Shorts are usually caught in a corner, and mostly they can cover their obligations only through private settlement with the interests creating the corner. The Stock Exchange does not permit corners. It is specified that a free and open market must be maintained in stock at all times.

COVERING—The buying back of stock sold short.

CREDIT BALANCE—The balance in favor of the customer on the broker's books.

CUMULATIVE—A class of preferred stock that must pay its stipulated dividend some time. If the company cannot pay the dividend when it falls due, the payment cannot be eliminated, but must go over to the time when the company can pay it. A corporation must pay back dividends on its cumulative preferred stock before it can make a distribution on its common stock.

DEBENTURE—A security generally supposed to be in the bond class, but unsecured by mortgage. It takes precedence over preferred and common stock.

DEBIT BALANCE—The amount the customer owes the broker.

DEFAULT—Failure of a corporation to pay interest due on its bonded debt.

DEFICIT—Where the income falls short of expenses and requirements.

DIGESTED SECURITIES—Newly created securities properly absorbed by the investing public.

DISCRETIONARY ACCOUNT—Where a speculator permits somebody else to do his trading for him without orders. This is highly dangerous and unsatisfactory. The Stock Exchange frowns on the practice. Large brokerage houses often refuse to accept such accounts.

DISTRIBUTION—The unloading on the public of stock that professionals have bought cheap. This is usually being done when the market looks strong.

DRIVE—An attempt by bear traders to make a sudden raid on the market, or an attempt by the bulls to drive the bears to cover.

DUMMY—One person acting in the place of another who wants to conceal his identity. Sometimes a director is a dummy serving an unknown master. Stock sometimes is in a dummy name when secret operations are being put through.

EQUITY—The difference between money loaned on securities and their market value.

EX-DIVIDEND—When the transfer books are closed for dividend purposes, a stock sells ex-dividend. That is, the amount of the dividend is knocked off the price on the Exchange.

FACE VALUE—The value of securities as printed on the certificate.

FEVERISH—The high-strung, nervous, and excited condition of an uncertain market, when it may plunge down any minute under panicky selling.

FIRM BID OR OFFER—A definite bid or offer binding upon the maker within a reasonable time.

FISCAL YEAR—The twelve-month period at the end of which a company balances its books. It may not be the calendar year.

FLOATING DEBT—Indebtedness payable within a short time.

FLOATING SUPPLY—The stock in circulation in Wall Street brokerage houses; the stock readily obtainable for speculative purposes.

FLOOR MAN—The employee of a stock-exchange commission house who handles your orders.

FLOOR TRADER—Members of the Stock Exchange who buy and sell for their own account. These floor traders are the real professionals.

FLURRY—A sudden and short-lived fluctuation in stock prices caused by an unexpected piece of news.

FLYER—A plunge into the stock-market on impulse. A dangerous gamble with the odds against the speculator.

FORCED SALE—A sale of stock against the inclinations of the holder, usually because of inability to produce more margin.

FUTURES—Trading in the cotton or grain market in contracts for future delivery. These contracts are speculated in like stock.

GILT-EDGED—A high-class security; one in which the risk is very small.

GOOD DELIVERY—A stock that complies with all the regulations of the Stock Exchange.

G.T.C.—An order to buy or sell, given by a customer, that is good on the broker's books until cancelled by order. The letters mean "Good till canceled."

G.T.M.—An order with the broker "Good this month."

G.T.W.—An order with the broker "Good this week."

GUARANTEED STOCK—Stock upon which the dividends and sometimes the principal are guaranteed. Some of the older railroad stocks are guaranteed, often by another company.

HEDGING—Buying one stock and selling another stock at the same time in an effort to guarantee against loss either way. A purely gambling operation.

HOLDING THE BAG—Of the operator who assumes final responsibility for a stock. When a speculator finds himself buying stock nobody else wants.

HONEYCOMBED MARKET—Where there are numerous stop orders placed below current quotations to protect margin accounts.

HYPOTHECATED—A trader hypothecates his securities when he deposits them with his broker as collateral.

INACTIVE STOCKS—Those that rarely come to market and therefore are not often seen on the stock ticker tape.

INDUSTRIALS—Shares of the large manufacturing companies.

INFLATION—Stocks that are selling above their intrinsic worth are said to be inflated.

INVESTMENT BUYING—Purchasing of stocks by that part of the public which is buying to hold and to secure an income return.

INVESTMENT SECURITIES—Those seasoned issues of good strong corporations that pay a dividend and have a long dividend record.

INVOLUNTARY INVESTOR—One who buys at the top and can't get rid of his stock without taking a loss.

JOINT ACCOUNT—Where two or more persons pool their resources to buy stock. This is a very unsatisfactory practice from any angle.

KITING—Pushing stocks to unwarranted high levels.

LAMB—A greenhorn or inexperienced trader.

LIMITED ORDERS—Orders on which a limit is placed by a trader with his broker on the price at which he will buy or sell stocks.

LISTED—Those stocks that are listed on one or another of the stock exchanges.

LOADED—When a trader is carrying all the stock he can buy with his resources. A dangerous position to be in.

LOAN CROWD—Refers to brokers who make a practice of loaning stock on the floor of the Exchange. By watching activities of the loan crowd a good idea of the short interest in the market can be gained.

LONG—When a trader buys stock and carries it, he is "long" of the market.

MANIPULATION—Controlling the movements of stocks by artificial methods. This is mostly done to attract the public and to unload stocks.

MARGIN—The money put up by the customer in part payment of the stock he wants to buy. The broker borrowing at his bank provides the balance of the purchase-price.

MARKET POSITION—The advantageous or disadvantageous position a speculator finds himself in.

MARKING UP—The process of advancing stocks in the market used by pools.

MELON—A bonus or division of profits by a corporation to its stockholders.

MERGER—A combination of companies under one management.

MILKING—When unscrupulous officers and directors of corporations pay themselves exorbitant salaries and squeeze all the money they can out of the treasury, it is called "milking the company."

NARROW MARKET—When price fluctuations are small and there is little difference between the high and low prices of the day.

ODD LOT—Any order under a hundred shares.

ON BID OR OFFER—When an odd-lot trader wants to buy or sell an active stock he can buy on the offering price or sell on the bid without waiting for an actual transaction to take place.

OPEN ORDER—An order placed with a broker to be filled when opportunity presents itself. In other words, good till canceled.

OVER-THE-COUNTER—The telephone market where stocks and bonds are dealt in that are not listed on any exchange. An enormous volume of securities are dealt in every day over the telephone in a market made between the offices of unlisted brokers.

PAPER PROFITS—The stuff dreams are made of. These are profits that show for the moment on the broker's books, but before the stock is sold out, may disappear or be turned into a loss. A profit is only a profit when the cash is in hand. It is a bad practice to spend paper profits.

PAR—The face value of a security.

PASSED—Refers to a dividend that is not paid when due.

PEGGED—Where a pool puts in a blanket order to buy all stock at a certain price to prevent its going to lower prices. This was done in several stocks during the crash of the fall of 1929. The pool is then holding the bag and taking all offerings.

PIT—The wheat pit in Chicago.

PLUNGER—One who speculates wildly and without forethought.

POINT—A point on the stock exchange is one dollar.

PREMIUM—When a stock sells above par, it is said to be at a premium. Many stocks have no par value.

PROXY—A legal document giving the right to vote at meetings. This right can be conferred on another person by a stockholder.

PUT—The opposite of a call. An agreement whereby the man who issues the put guarantees to give the holder the privilege of delivering to him a specified stock at a specified price within a certain period. The put is sold several points below the prevailing market price. The man who buys it believes that within the life of the put the market will decline and he will be able to buy the specified stock lower than the price at which the maker of the put will have to take it from him.

PYRAMIDING—The risky practice of buying additional stock on paper profits. A trader is permitted by his broker to buy stock with profits that have not yet been collected. The paper profit is recognized as margin.

PREFERRED STOCK—Stock that has the first claim on the company's assets after the bonds and before the common stock.

RAID—A sudden coup by the bears who attack a market that has been weakened by over-speculation on the bull side.

RAILS—Shares of the railroad companies.

RALLY—A quick recovery in prices after a decline.

REACTION—A reversal of the upward trend in prices. The temporary halting of a bull movement.

REALIZING—Profit taking by speculative bull traders. This selling sometimes causes a reaction.

RIGHTS—The privilege given to a holder of stock to subscribe to new stock of the same corporation. Sometimes the old stockholders are given the first right to subscribe.

RIGGING THE MARKET—Building up false price structure to attract buying.

SCALE—Stocks may be bought or sold on a scale up or down. A large order broken up into smaller transactions to be executed at stipulated prices, usually with several points between orders.

SCALPING—Trading for small profits.

SCRIP—A certificate for a fractional part of a stock.

SEASONING—The evolution of a stock from the doubtful to the investment class. The maturing of a stock.

SELLER'S OPTION—An agreement whereby the seller of a stock need not make a delivery until a specified time.

SEMI-SPECULATIVE—Not a hundred per cent investment. An investment with a certain risk attached to it.

SHAKING THE TREE—The time-honored custom of professionals' making the market look weak to frighten timid speculators out of the market.

SHORT—One who has sold stock he does not own.

SHORT COVERING—Buying by shorts to make delivery.

SHORT INTEREST—Refers to the number of shorts in the market.

SKY-ROCKETING—Rising of stocks to dizzy heights. The danger signal for amateur traders.

SLUGGISH MARKET—Dull trading with little speculative interest.

SOFT MARKET—Inclined to be weak. Stocks have to be sold at concessions.

SOLD OUT—When it becomes necessary for the broker to sell his clients' securities to protect himself against loss.

SPECIALIST—Broker who handles orders in one or more stocks for other brokers.

SPECULATION—Webster's Dictionary defines it as "To buy or sell with the expectation of profiting by a rise or fall in price; often to engage in hazardous business transactions for the chance of unusually large profit." The dictionary also defines "speculation" as "Intuition; vision; reasoning taking the form of prolonged and systematic analysis."

SPOT TRANSACTION—Term used in the commodity markets meaning immediate delivery.

SPOTTY MARKET—A condition where some stocks are advancing while others are declining.

SPURT—A sudden and unexpected jump forward in the price of one or more stocks.

SQUEEZE—When shorts are compelled to buy back because of strong buying and advancing prices.

STANDARD STOCKS—Those of well-known corporations.

STEELS—Shares of the steel-manufacturers listed on the Exchange.

STOCK DIVIDEND—A dividend paid by a corporation in stock instead of cash. Sometimes a stock dividend is in the nature of a melon or a bonus.

STOCK-JOBBING—Circulating false news and information pertaining to a certain stock.

STOP LOSS ORDER—Order to sell placed by cautious traders just under the purchase-price to guard against loss in case of a decline. Stop orders are automatically executed by specialists.

STREET NAME—A certificate is said to be in a "Street name" when the certificate is issued to and endorsed by a member of the Exchange.

STREET STOCK—Stock that is afloat in brokerage houses.

SUPPORTING ORDERS—Usually buying orders placed by powerful banking interests to bolster up the market in times of trouble.

SYNDICATE—A group of bankers combined to finance a corporation through the wholesale purchase of its securities. The syndicate resells the securities to the public at a profit.

TAKE UP—To pay the balance owed on the purchase-price of securities.

TECHNICAL CONDITION—The internal condition of the market regardless of surface indications.

TIME MONEY—That loaned for long periods. Distinct from call money.

TIP—Something to be avoided.

TOP-HEAVY MARKET—One that is overbought, in which prices are inflated. The market that gives the bear a happy hunting-ground.

TRADING LIST—The securities that are bought and sold on the Exchange.

TREASURY STOCK—Unissued stock still in the treasury.

TURN—Buying for a quick turn. The turn usually is the wrong way.

UNDERTONE—The real condition of the market.

UNLOADING—Professionals' disposing of stocks to the lambs.

WASH SALE—Where a person buys and sells the identical stock at the same time to maintain a market. He is buying from himself and selling to himself. Such transactions are forbidden by the Stock Exchange. Any broker caught at it would be expelled.

WATERED—A corporation is said to be watered when the outstanding stock far exceeds the assets.

WEAK HOLDINGS—Stock held on margin by people with limited capital who will sell on the slightest provocation.

WHEN, AS, AND IF—Stocks dealt in before they are actually issued by a corporation are bought and sold on the understanding "when, as, and if issued."

GOLDEN RULES

Pay all bills before speculating.

Don't speculate with another person's money.

Don't neglect your business to speculate.

If the market makes you irritable or interferes with sleep, you are wrong.

Don't use in the market money that you need for other purposes.

Don't go "joint account" with a friend—play a lone hand.

Don't give a broker "discretionary powers." If you can't run your own account, leave the market alone.

The broker who demands a large margin is your friend. Only a bucket-shop wants you to trade on a slender margin.

Don't buy more stock than you can safely carry. Over-trading means forced selling and losses.

Get accurate information. Demand facts, not opinions.

Don't take advice from uninformed people—they know no more than you about the market.

Such advice as "I think well of it" or "It is a cinch" means nothing.

Use only a part of your capital in speculation.

Don't buy "cats and dogs" (unseasoned stocks).

Buy good standard stocks that have stood the test of time.

Remember that good stocks always come back—unknown stocks may disappear.

Don't buy in a hurry—there is plenty of time to buy good stocks.

Investigate each stock thoroughly before you buy.

Remember that it is easier to buy than to sell. The salability of a stock is very important.

The market moves up slowly, but goes down fast.

Be prepared to buy your stock outright if necessary. If you can't do this, you are taking chances.

Buy in a selling market—when nobody wants stock.

Sell in a buying market—when everybody wants stock.

The market is most dangerous when it looks best; it is most inviting when it looks worst.

Don't get too active. Many trades, many losses.

Long-pull trades are most profitable.

Don't try to outguess the market.

Look out for the buying fever; it is a dangerous disease.

Don't try to pick the top and the bottom of the market.

Don't dream in the stock-market; have some idea just how far your stock can go.

Remember that the majority of traders are always buying at the top and selling at the bottom.

Don't worry over the profits you might have made.

Don't spend your paper profits—they might turn into losses.

Watch the news. Remember that the market actually is a barometer of business and credit.

Don't buy fads or novelties—be sure the company you are becoming a partner in makes something everybody wants.

Don't finance new inventions unless you are wealthy.

Ask who manages the company whose stock you want to buy.

Don't follow pool operations. The pools are out to get you.

Don't listen to or give tips. Good tips are scarce and they take a long time to materialize.

Don't take flyers.

Don't treat your losses lightly; they are serious. You are losing actual currency.

When you win, don't get reckless; put your winnings in the bank for a while.

Don't talk about the market—you will attract too much idle gossip.

Sniff at inside information; it is usually bunk. The big people don't talk about their operations.

Don't speculate unless you have plenty of time to think about it.

Fortunes are not easily made in Wall Street. Some professionals give their lives to the market and die poor.

There is such a thing as luck, but it does not hold all the time.

Don't pyramid.

Don't average unless you are sure you know your stock.

Don't buy more stock than you can afford, just to look big. If you are a ten-share man, don't be ashamed of it.

Beware of a stock that is given an abundance of publicity.

Use your mistakes as object-lessons—the person who makes the same mistake twice deserves no sympathy.

Don't open an account at the broker's just to oblige a friend. Charity and speculation don't mix.

Remember that many people believe they can find better use for your money than you can yourself.

Leave short selling to experienced professionals.

If you must sell short, pick a widely held stock or you may get caught in a corner.

Money made easily in the market is never valued— easy come, easy go.

Don't blame the Stock Exchange for your own mistakes.

Don't shape your financial policy on what your barber advises—hundreds of experts are waiting to give you exact information.

Don't let emotion or prejudice warp your judgment. Base your operations on facts.

Some Standard Stocks Listed on the New York Stock Exchange

Allied Chemical and Dye
American Can
American Power and Light
American Radiator
American Smelting
American Telephone and Telegraph
American Tobacco
Anaconda Copper
Atchison Railroad
Baldwin Locomotive
Bethlehem Steel
Borden Company
Canadian Pacific Railroad
Consolidated Gas
Corn Products
Delaware and Hudson Railroad
Eastman Kodak
General Electric
General Motors
International Telephone and Telegraph
Kennecott Copper
National Biscuit
National Lead
New York Central

North American Company
Otis Elevator
Paramount
Pennsylvania Railroad
Public Service of New Jersey
Pullman Corporation
Radio Corporation of America
Standard Brands
Standard Oil of New Jersey
Texas Corporation
United Gas Improvement
Union Pacific
United States Steel
Westinghouse Electric
Woolworth

COSIMO is an innovative publisher of books and publications that inspire, inform and engage readers worldwide. Our titles are drawn from a range of subjects including health, business, philosophy, history, science and sacred texts. We specialize in using print-on-demand technology (POD), making it possible to publish books for both general and specialized audiences and to keep books in print indefinitely. With POD technology new titles can reach their audiences faster and more efficiently than with traditional publishing.

> **Permanent Availability:** Our books & publications never go out-of-print.

> **Global Availability:** Our books are always available online at popular retailers and can be ordered from your favorite local bookstore.

COSIMO CLASSICS brings to life unique, rare, out-of-print classics representing subjects as diverse as *Alternative Health, Business and Economics, Eastern Philosophy, Personal Growth, Mythology, Philosophy, Sacred Texts, Science, Spirituality* and much more!

COSIMO-on-DEMAND publishes your books, publications and reports. If you are an Author, part of an Organization, or a Benefactor with a publishing project and would like to bring books back into print, publish new books fast and effectively, would like your publications, books, training guides, and conference reports to be made available to your members and wider audiences around the world, we can assist you with your publishing needs.

Visit our website at www.cosimobooks.com to learn more about Cosimo, browse our catalog, take part in surveys or campaigns, and sign-up for our newsletter.

And if you wish please drop us a line at info@cosimobooks.com. We look forward to hearing from you.

CPSIA information can be obtained
at www.ICGtesting.com
Printed in the USA
BVOW08s2235061117
499706BV00001B/7/P